'LIVE AND
LET OTHERS
LIVE'

'LIVE AND LET OTHERS LIVE'

~

LIFE LESSONS FROM
MAHAVIRA

EDITED BY
Nanditha Krishna

ALEPH

ALEPH

ALEPH BOOK COMPANY
An independent publishing firm
promoted by *Rupa Publications India*

First published in India in 2019
by Aleph Book Company
7/16 Ansari Road, Daryaganj
New Delhi 110 002

Series Introduction Copyright © Nanditha Krishna 2019
Book Introduction Copyright © Nanditha Krishna 2019
This Edition Copyright © Aleph Book Company 2019
Copyright for individual pieces vests with respective
authors

ISBN: 978-93-88292-42-9

1 3 5 7 9 10 8 6 4 2

Printed and bound in India by Replika Press Pvt. Ltd.

EDITOR'S NOTE

I have always revered Mahavira, a great saint of India who made the ideal of compassion and non-violence the basis of his teachings over 2,500 years ago. As an activist for animals and the environment, I cannot think of a greater role model. The opportunity to write about him was heaven-sent, but since I don't know Prakrit, I couldn't delve into the original texts. Fortunately, good friends came to my rescue. Dr Priyadarshana Jain of Madras University introduced me to works on Bhagwan Mahavira. Shri D. R. Mehta, founder of Bhagwan Mahaveer Viklang Sahayata Samiti, gave me the *Samana Sutta*, which encapsulates Jain philosophy. Most importantly, Shri Dulichand Jain, President of Karuna International, Chennai, which teaches compassion and kindness towards animals to children worldwide, not only gave me his many books of aphorisms translated from the Jain sutras but also gave me blanket permission to use them, and read and commented on what I had written. Many of the aphorisms are taken from his books and edited by me for the lay reader. My sincere thanks to all of them for sharing their knowledge with me.

SERIES INTRODUCTION

India has produced some of the world's greatest religious leaders, sages, saints, philosophers and spiritual thinkers. They were monks, nuns and renunciates, nationalists and reformers. No one religion had a monopoly on them. They range from Mahavira and Buddha, who lived over 2,500 years ago, to medieval saints like Chishti, Avvaiyar and Guru Nanak, to more recent philosophers and religious icons such as Vivekananda, Ramakrishna, Saint Teresa and many others. Each of them touched the lives of the people they lived among and the generations that followed. They inspired devotees and followers with their erudition and wisdom. The spiritual and philosophical heritage they left behind is India's gift to all Indians and the world.

Through the 'Life Lessons' series we will examine the teachings of some of India's best-known spiritual teachers. Each book will be a handy companion to help the reader along the difficult pathways of life.

Happiness and sorrow are unavoidable. The world is a place of trials and problems recur in every generation. Is suffering a necessary part of human life? How can one overcome suffering? Can hardship make a person stronger? What is happiness? Everybody wants to be happy, but how does one achieve this state? Does happiness come from vast riches and great achievements or does it come from the satisfaction of the soul? Is worldly success more important or is it fulfilment that one should seek?

These and similar questions vex every individual and have preoccupied the minds of philosophers and religious savants down the ages. The answers that these great souls found to life's conundrums occupy entire libraries worth of books and texts. This series is culled from their essential teachings and will present to readers some of the greatest truths to be found in India's spiritual heritage in a simple and accessible way. It is to be hoped that what you find here will prompt you to go deeper into the life and work of those who plumbed life's greatest mysteries.

Walking in the footsteps of these great men and women can take each of us to greater heights of knowledge, wisdom and understanding. They can teach us how to find happiness and peace and the true meaning of well-being and success. Most of all, they can teach us how to value one another and cherish the holy gift of life.

INTRODUCTION

Mahavira was a sixth-century reformer and philosopher, the twenty-fourth Tirthankara of the Jains who established Jainism as a new faith. He was a prince, born to inherit and rule. Yet, one day, Prince Vardhamana left home, abandoning his kingdom and his wealth, to become an ascetic. What prompted him to leave? Was it an inner calling? Or was it hearing the piteous cries of goats that were being readied for slaughter?

Mahavira (who was born Vardhamana in the sixth century BCE) was the son of King Siddhartha of Kundagrama (near Patna in present-day Bihar) and his wife Trishala or Priyakarni, daughter of King Chetaka of Vaishali. Siddhartha belonged to the Ikshvaku lineage of Shri Rama of Ayodhya. Before Vardhamana's birth, Queen Trishala had fourteen auspicious dreams, signifying that the child was destined for greatness. As per Shwetambara texts, Vardhamana was married to Yashoda, daughter of Samaravira, a great warrior, and had a daughter named Priyadarshana or Anojja. According to the Digambara texts, however, he never married.

Mahavira is credited with several miracles. Once, as a child, he was playing with his friends when a cobra appeared. The other children picked up stones, and cried, 'Kill it.' But young Vardhamana sat down and extended his hand to the snake. The cobra crawled up his arm until it was at eye level with him. The two gazed at each other and then played together like friends. Finally, Vardhamana left the cobra on a tree and bade him goodbye.

Vardhamana was a prince, brought up to rule and live a life of power and luxury. But he constantly thought about deeper philosophical concepts. He asked his teacher whether his body and soul were separate entities, whether the mind could be controlled, and so on. Finally, his teacher told him that while the school could teach him about warfare and politics, he would have to find answers to his philosophical questions elsewhere. Vardhamana left the school and returned to the palace. Gradually, he started withdrawing from the world. He began searching for the absolute Truth and the answer to the question—Who am I?

At the age of thirty, this young prince abandoned his kingdom, palace and family and renounced the world. He was sent off in a palanquin in a majestic procession befitting royalty. He then cast off his royal vestments in preference for a single white cloth befitting a shramana or one who performs austerities.

Vardhamana (prosperous) now became Mahavira (brave). He underwent rigorous austerities and penance for twelve years. The new appellation was appropriate, considering the stringent practices he subjected himself to. After thirteen months, he discarded even the white cloth and put himself through severe physical and mental hardships to develop detachment from the body. He endured extreme temperatures of heat and cold. He was mocked, beaten and tortured, had insults and atrocities heaped on him by people, was bitten by insects and starved for several months. The tortures he suffered were terrible, but he bore them in silence, for it was his path to the Truth. He was in deep sadhana and so detached from his body that he could no longer feel pain or pleasure. Nothing could distract him from his sadhana. His soul became the observer, as did his senses, mind and body. He now identified himself as a bhikkhu or mendicant and was totally detached from the world.

Mahavira spent twelve years pursuing a life of penance to conquer his basic attachments. He went into maunavrat (vow of silence), practising complete silence and rigorous meditation. He sought to overcome negative emotions like anger and derive a calm and peaceful demeanour. He moved from one place to another, hardly sleeping, and fasting most of the time. During his years of penance, he travelled through modern-day Bihar, Bengal, Odisha and Uttar Pradesh.

After the passage of twelve years, Mahavira fell asleep for a few moments and dreamt ten unusual dreams, the meanings and significance of which have been explained in the Jain scriptures.

In the first dream, Mahavira saw himself defeating a lion, signifying the conquest of moha or attachment. The next was a white-feathered bird, which signified that Mahavira had achieved purity of mind. The third was a bird with multi-coloured feathers which denoted his multifaceted knowledge. His fourth dream was of two strings of gems, which symbolized the duality of his preaching—for the monk and the householder. He then saw a herd of cows which signified his devoted followers. This was followed by a pond with blooming lotuses, symbolic of celestial spirits that would promulgate his cause. He then saw himself swimming across the ocean, signifying freedom from the cycle of life, death and rebirth. Next, he saw radiant sunrays spreading in all directions, implying that he would attain kevala jnana or omniscience. After this, he saw himself encircling a mountain with his intestines, which meant that the universe would share his knowledge. The tenth dream was of him sitting on a throne atop Mount Meru, signifying his reverence for knowledge and that Mahavira was now in the highest position of respect.

Finally, on the tenth day of the waxing moon in the month of Vaishakha, in 557 BCE, Mahavira sat under a sala tree on the banks of the Rijuvaluka River and attained kevala jnana. He had attained perfect vision, understanding, knowledge, conduct, and bliss. He became a jina (conqueror), arhat (worshipful) and kevali (all-knowing). Mahavira—now Bhagavan Mahavira—became the twenty-fourth Tirthankara of the Nirgrantha school.

The word Tirthankara means a ford-maker and signifies one who has crossed the sea of samsara, liberated from the cycle of births, deaths and rebirths. He is the supreme teacher of dharma—the path of righteousness. The first Jain Tirthankara was Adinatha or Rishabhanatha. The Yajur Veda mentions the names of Rishabha, Ajitanatha and Arishtanemi, three Tirthankaras who came before Mahavira. The Jains believe that the twenty-second Tirthankara, Neminatha, was a cousin of Lord Krishna. The twenty-third Tirthankara, who preceded Mahavira, was Parshvanatha. During the period preceding Mahavira, the Jain religion was known as Arhata Dharma, a name by which it is still known in many places. During the time of Mahavira, the faith became known as Nirgrantha.

Every Tirthankara goes through five stages in his life: conception, when he enters his mother's womb; birth, when he enters the world; renunciation, when he becomes an ascetic; kevali, when he attains omniscience and becomes a preacher; and nirvana, when he reaches final liberation. After attaining kevala jnana, it is believed that the Tirthankara begins preaching in the samavasarana, a heavenly pavilion where gods, people and animals assemble to hear him. Each Tirthankara is represented by an animal, or occasionally by a plant or other symbols. Mahavira's emblem was the lion, a symbol of royalty.

Having attained omniscience, Mahavira began preaching as he wandered from one place to another on foot. He reached Pava, the kingdom of Raja Hastipala, in time for a grand animal sacrifice to be presided over by a famous Brahmin named Indrabhuti Gautama. As the crowds moved towards the visiting

Mahavira, Indrabhuti was curious and went to see this arihant, a man who had conquered his inner passions of attachment, anger, pride and greed and had realized his pure self. Fascinated, Indrabhuti did not return to the sacrifice but stayed on to listen. He was soon joined by his brothers Agnibhuti and Vayubhuti. The three of them became the ganadharas or chief disciples. Mahavira acquired eight more disciples, including Vyaktabhuti, Sudharma, Manditaputra, Mauryaputra, Akampita, Achalabhrata, Metraya and Prabhasa, all of whom were Brahmins. A ganadhara had to be of exceptional brilliance in order to fully comprehend and interpret the divine teachings of a Tirthankara. At his very first sermon, Mahavira acquired eleven ganadharas, former Brahmins and practitioners of sacrificial rites, along with their followers.

Mahavira also ordained nuns, the first being Chandana, granddaughter of King Chetaka who was Mahavira's maternal grandfather. Ordaining women was not unknown at the time as the Shaivas had done so long before the Jains and Buddhists. The ordination of Chandana opened the floodgates and thousands of women—nobles and commoners—came forward to be ordained under the leadership of Chandana.

Mahavira believed that gender and caste did not determine a person's greatness—a soul became great by its actions. He encouraged people from all walks of life—royalty and commoners, the rich and the poor, men and women, high castes and untouchables—to participate in his dharma and ordained them all without discrimination. He believed that all are equally capable of attaining moksha and must therefore be equally respected and revered.

The ultimate goal of life, according to Mahavira, was to attain freedom from the cycle of birth, death and rebirth, as human life is one of pain and suffering. Every living being suffers from the fetters of karma, which is the accumulation of one's deeds in this and previous births. The soul is eternal, neither created nor destructible. The life of each soul is determined by one's karma. Good actions liberate the soul, while bad ones imprison it forever. People seek pleasure in material possessions that result in evils such as greed, anger, violence and self-centredness. These result in the accumulation of bad karma which does not permit the soul to be liberated.

Mahavira believed that there is no superior power that controls our destiny or causes us to be happy or unhappy. We weave our own fortunes—good or bad—and are responsible for our own destinies. We can extricate ourselves from the cycle of birth, death and rebirth by effort and determination. Awareness of this power is self-realization. Once the difference between the self and the physical body is experienced, the path to freedom of the soul begins, and this freedom is the ultimate happiness. The idea that the physical body is the self is misguided.

In due course, Mahavira established the chaturvidha sangha or four-fold congregation consisting of ordained monks (sadhus) and nuns (sadhvis), laymen or householders (shravaks) and laywomen (shravikas). He laid down a clear organizational structure for the sangha with distinct responsibilities for each position.

The monks (also called shramanas) and nuns (also known as shramanis) were expected to spend their time in contemplation and self-discipline. They had to give up all material possessions and practise celibacy. They were expected to travel on foot from one place to another to teach people how they could liberate their soul. They vowed to live a simple and sin-free life, to avoid impure thoughts and actions, and dedicate themselves to the liberation of the soul. Every monk and nun had to observe the five great vows enunciated by Mahavira: ahimsa or non-violence, satya or truth, asteya or non-stealing, brahmacharya or chastity and aparigraha or non-attachment. They had to be obedient to the head of the order. From begging for alms, to taking medical treatment, to their duties at a time of calamity, they had to respect their preceptor whose instructions were supreme. The seeker of truth was called a sadhaka and was required to avoid thoughts and actions that were impure and sinful. For those unable to keep their vows, Mahavira suggested atonement by undertaking harsh penance over punishment. By atonement, the path reopened for the sadhaka to continue his or her spiritual quest towards kevala jnana. Everyone who joined the sangha had to respect, honour, help and obey all other sadhakas. The Jain path of purification comprised fourteen stages of spiritual progress. Arhat is the thirteenth stage, when the soul is free of past karma and the sadhaka achieves absolute consciousness and knowledge or kevala jnana.

Laypersons (householders) were also welcome in the sangha and could become laymen (shravaks) and laywomen (shravikas). While their primary responsibility was to their families, they were also responsible for the well-being of the community. Householders had to observe anuvratas (minor vows) and serve ascetics by providing food and alms, temporary residence for visiting monks and nuns and propagate the philosophy of the shramanas, as the followers of Mahavira came to be known. Charity of four kinds was expected from householders: food, medicine, scriptural teachings and protection to all living beings.

Mahavira preached his sacred doctrines for thirty years and was able to attract several kings of his time. King Bimbisara of Magadha (558–491 BCE) who was a follower of the Buddha was attracted by Mahavira's teachings and became a Jain, impressed by the calmness of a Jain monk. He frequently visited the samavasarana of Mahavira, seeking answers to his queries. Bimbisara's second wife, Chellana, a princess of Vaishali and daughter of King Chetaka, Mahavira's maternal grandfather, was Mahavira's ardent disciple. King Chetaka contributed greatly to the growth of the Jain religion among the kings of modern-day Uttar Pradesh and Bihar.

At the age of seventy-two Mahavira reached Pava where he stayed in the garden of King Hastipala. In 527 BCE (according to the Shwetambaras; 510 BCE according to the Digambaras), his soul left his body to begin its final journey—this day is celebrated as Mahavira's mahanirvana or Diwali. Nine of his eleven ganadharas had already passed away and only Indrabhuti and Sudharma lived. Indrabhuti died within a few hours of his teacher. The Kalpa Sutra describes Mahavira's passing beautifully:

On that night when the venerable ascetic Mahavira attained nirvana, cutting asunder the ties of birth, old age and death, became a siddha, thus finally liberated... (Kalpa Sutra, 126)

And on that night during which the venerable ascetic Mahavira obtained nirvana, the eighteen confederate kings of Kasi and Kosala, the Mallas and Licchavis instituted an illumination with lighted lamps for, they said, 'since the internal light is gone, let us make an illumination with the external light of matter'. (Kalpa Sutra, 127)

THE PHILOSOPHY OF MAHAVIRA

Arhata Dharma existed before Mahavira, whose teachings were based on those of the preceding Tirthankaras. Unlike the Buddha, who was the founder of a new faith, Mahavira reformed and propagated the beliefs of an existing religious order. He himself followed the teachings of his predecessor Parshvanatha. Although Mahavira was the last Tirthankara of

Jainism, he was responsible for establishing Jainism as a religion. While the Buddha preached in Pali, Mahavira preferred Ardha Magadhi Prakrit. Mahavira's sermons were compiled by Indrabhuti Gautama and transmitted to the common people orally. But they are believed to have been largely lost by about the first century CE when they were first written down. The surviving versions of the Agamas or Agama Sutras form the basic texts of Jainism.

The philosophy of Mahavira consists of eight cardinal principles—three metaphysical and five ethical. According to the metaphysical principles, the universe exists eternally, for it was never created, nor can it be destroyed. It is made up of six eternal substances: souls, space, time, material atoms, medium of motion and medium of rest. These components are independent of each other and undergo change to create the reality with its many facets in which uninitiated mortals exist.

Of the ethical principles, ahimsa or non-violence is the first vow, which is fundamental to Jainism. Every living being is subject to the laws of karma—birth, death and rebirth—and in order to renounce that cycle, ahimsa or non-violence is the most important principle. If that is not followed, all other good deeds and principles are useless. A good person, lay or ascetic, should never harm any living being by thought, word or deed. The Upanishadic dictum—ahimsa paramo dharmah (non-violence is the greatest Truth)—saw its apogee in the teachings of Mahavira. He taught that all life in any form—human and animal—must be protected from violence and injury. This is the fundamental duty of a Jain.

Violence, said Mahavira, is of two types—unintentional violence resulting from the actions of the body and intentional violence motivated by the mind. Although the actions of the body are inevitable acts of survival, our conscience must be aware of the violence we commit, be aware of excesses and seek pardon from those we hurt. This is because violence hurts the soul of the person committing the sin, collecting karmas and thereby hurting its chances of liberation. Animal sacrifices, killing animals for food, fishing, hunting and similar acts of violence merely satisfy the ugly needs of the human mind and are not acts of survival. Kindness and compassion are natural to the soul, not killing. Passions are invariably involved in the conduct of violence and form strong karmic bonds, violating the soul. Violence is of many types: lying, exploiting others, depriving another of his livelihood or legitimate rights, being oblivious to the pain and suffering of others, treating another as an inferior being, and denying education or knowledge. Poverty, child labour, and discriminating against a person on the basis of gender or caste are acts of violence too, said Mahavira. Non-violence is not for those who wish to stay quiet in the face of violence and injustice, nor is it for cowards. Bhava himsa is mental violence and can only be changed by changing mental attitudes. One must work individually or collectively to serve others and eliminate himsa. Those who live a life helping others without any expectation of reward (the nishkama karma of the Bhagavad Gita), without attachment or passion, live a life of serenity and happiness. Peace and tranquillity come from pure, non-violent attitudes of the mind.

Escaping the cycle of birth and death should be the goal of every person. However, even greater is the mitigation of pain and suffering of all living beings. Serving humanity, bringing justice to all people, spreading humaneness and ensuring that no one commits violence or himsa is the definitive path to the liberation of the soul. Mahavira wanted his followers to become the motivators, leaders and emissaries of ahimsa. A good ruler, he continued, should be disciplined, make friends, make peace, and co-operate with other rulers to provide security and comfort to all creation.

Vegetarianism, a natural corollary of ahimsa, is absolutely essential to Jainism. Milk and milk products may be consumed only if they are produced without harming the cow. Root vegetables such as potatoes, onions, garlic, carrots, etc. are avoided because tiny organisms are injured when the plant is pulled out. Further, the root is seen as the source of life of the plant itself and pulling it out is akin to killing the plant. It is not uncommon to see Jain sadhus and sadhvis with their mouths covered with a white cloth to prevent insects from going in and being consumed accidentally, or sweeping the ground in front of them as they walk, in order to avoid stepping on an insect or any other organism, however small. Further, Jains are discouraged from eating after sunset and before sunrise because they may accidentally consume small organisms which could have fallen into their food. This would have been particularly important in an age when there was no electric lighting.

Today, India is home to the highest number of vegetarians in the world. If the Brahmins became vegetarians over the course of over two and a half millennia, it may be ascribed to Mahavira, who made vegetarianism into the greatest virtue that a person may possess and essential for the soul to reach a state of moksha or liberation.

Satya or truth is the second vow: never tell a lie nor speak a falsehood for any reason whatsoever, said the great master. Further, do not encourage or approve of any person who tells a lie. Truth in Mahavira's teachings was not merely the great Truth of the universe, but also the simple expedient of speaking the truth at all times.

Asteya or non-stealing—the third vow—is about more than the mere act of thieving. One should not desire or touch or take things that belong to others. Even the desire to own something belonging to someone else and taking it without permission is theft. Further, a monk should ask for permission to take, even if something is freely given.

The fourth vow is brahmacharya (celibacy), which is of two types. For a monk or nun, it involves total abstinence from sex and sensual pleasures. For a layperson, celibacy means loyalty to one's partner. Even coveting another woman (or man) is breaking the vow of celibacy.

The final vow, aparigraha or non-possession, is important, for desire and attachment are the root of all problems. An ascetic must renounce all property, possessions, family and relationships and own nothing. A monk or nun may not even stay in one place for

any length of time, except during the chaturmas.*
He must also renounce internal negativity, such as
anger, egotism, greed, likes and dislikes, attachments,
aversions, passions, etc. A layperson must limit his
possessions to what he needs for his personal use
and should not be attached to material goods. Every
Jain is required to take these five vows.

If the most important principle of Jainism is
ahimsa, the most important concept is anekaantavada
or many-sided realities. Anekaantavada is regard for
the viewpoints of others. It describes the plurality of
existence and teaches that truth and reality may differ
when perceived from different points of views. No
single view is absolute. There are infinite points of
view, each expressing a partial truth. Viewed together,
they represent the totality of all existence. The best
example is the tale of the five visually challenged men
who touched five different parts of the elephant. Each
described the elephant by the part of the body he had

---

*The holy four-month period from July to October when Hindu
and Jain monks and nuns perform penance, observe strict
austerities and spend their time fasting, meditating and praying.

touched, and each was partially right. The sum total of what the five men had touched was the absolute truth or, in that case, the elephant.

Mahavira encouraged his followers to have regard for the views of others in order to understand the absolute reality. Anekaantavada is intended to promote tolerance, create an atmosphere of mutual understanding and harmony and provide reconciliation.

However, even to promote an atmosphere of give-and-take, Mahavira absolutely refused to condone activities such as violence, killing animals for sacrifice or for food, or violence against other human beings. The five basic vows were indispensable.

The five elements—earth, air, fire, water and vegetation—or panchamahabhuta, which are the basis of all cosmic creation according to the philosophies of Hinduism, Jainism and Buddhism, must be respected and protected, for their existence is closely coalesced with ours. Mahavira emphasized the fundamental nature of symbiosis, or mutual interdependence, which forms the basis of ecological sciences today.

Parasparopagraho sarvajivanam (the binding together of all life by mutual support and interdependence) is an ancient Jain scriptural aphorism as valid today as it was 2,500 years ago. It is contemporary in its perspective, defining the scope of all ecology. All aspects of nature belong together and are bound together both physically and metaphysically. Mahavira encouraged his followers to sensitize the soul in order to receive the vibrations from every living being and understand nature.

Mahavira taught that self-discipline controls the senses and eliminates negative passions such as ego, anger, hatred, deceit, lust and greed. If we eliminate these passions, we eliminate sins—violence, lying, killing and hurting others. Sadhana or austerities enable the sadhaka to eliminate passions and attain control over the demands of the body. Sadhana, he said, must sensitize you to the sufferings of other living beings and serve the common good. Treat others as you would like to be treated. Be aware of the sufferings of all beings; serve them to alleviate their suffering. Do not fail to understand the difference between physical pleasure and eternal bliss. But Mahavira's sadhana went further, in that he believed that it should alleviate the pain and suffering of all creation.

The true path leading to liberation from the cycle of karma, according to Mahavira, is samyak darshana (right faith), samyak jnana (right knowledge) and samyak charitra (right conduct), three basic principles that were further elaborated as the twelve sacred scriptures, known as the twelve agamas, by the ganadhara Indrabhuti Gautama.

Dharma is the essential nature of any substance. The triple jewels—right faith, right knowledge and right conduct—comprise dharma and are the pathway to liberation. Giving protection to all living creatures is also dharma. The ten characteristics of dharma are supreme forgiveness, supreme humility, supreme straightforwardness, supreme truthfulness, supreme purity, supreme self-restraint, supreme austerity, supreme renunciation, supreme detachment and supreme continence.

Buddhists and Jains both denied the authority of the Vedas and the caste system based on birth.

They believed in compassion and ahimsa, a natural response to the excesses of Vedic animal sacrifices. Jainism accepts the existence of the eternal, non-material soul which persists through all changes and migrates from one body to another until it reaches the final state of liberation. Buddhism, on the other hand, denies the existence of such a soul, believing in an unbroken series of states each depending on the preceding one. Mahavira spoke of the existence of the soul but not of God. The soul has an independent progress and reaches the highest position after being purified by the destruction of attachment and hatred. It is a self-regulated absolute existence. Thus while Jainism follows the philosophy of non-creation of the universe by God, it believes in the cycle of birth, death and rebirth. This tradition is known Shramana (Samana in Pali and Prakrit) dharma.

SHWETAMBARA AND DIGAMBARA

The original doctrines of Jainism had been recorded in the fourteen Purva scriptures. Some 200 years after Mahavira, Chandragupta Maurya (321–297 BCE) the ruler of Magadha, followed his Jain preceptor Bhadrabahu to the south, to modern Karnataka, during a great famine in the kingdom. Sthulabhadra, another religious leader, remained in Magadha. Over the years, the knowledge of the doctrine was getting lost, so a council was called in Pataliputra, where eleven Anga scriptures were compiled and fourteen Purvas were included in the twelfth Anga by Sthulabhadra's followers. When Bhadrabahu's followers returned after the death of their preceptor, there was a dispute over the authenticity of the Angas. Meanwhile, those who had stayed back at Magadha had started wearing white clothes and were now known as Shwetambaras. This was unacceptable to those who had returned from their travels—they believed in discarding all clothes and remaining naked. Thus the naked Digambaras and the white-clad Shwetambaras became two sects. According to the Digambaras, the Purvas and the Angas were lost. About 980 to 993 years after the nirvana of Mahavira, a council was held at Vallabhi (now in Gujarat) which recorded the remaining Angas.

Digambara monks carry a broom made of fallen peacock feathers and a water gourd. They believe in attaining moksha through a life of strict penance and give up their clothes to symbolize freedom from worldly attachments. Shwetambaras believe that monks need not discard their clothes and that nudism is no longer practical.

The Digambaras believe that Mahavira never married and that after attaining enlightenment, Mahavira was free from human necessities like hunger, thirst, and sleep. According to Shwetambara texts, Mahavira did marry and father a child.

Women can obtain moksha according to the Shwetambaras, a state of the soul denied to women by the Digambaras. Some Shwetambara monks and nuns cover their mouth with a white cloth or mukhapatti in order to prevent even small insects from entering their mouths and thereby practise ahimsa all the time.

Fasting, mortification of the body, penance and other austerities are followed by both Digambaras and Shwetambaras in order to destroy past karma and prevent acquiring new ones. The soul must reach a state of siddha (the wise one) and, finally, moksha or liberation.

◆

Mahavira's love and compassion were universal and unconditional. His path to freedom for the soul was filled with selfless love. He never avoided questions, his knowledge had no limits. He was omniscient; his sadhana had achieved him the superior state of siddha. Contrary to popular perception, it was Mahavira and not the Buddha who halted the animal sacrifices of the Vedic religion. Ahimsa paramo dharmah...non-violence is the greatest Truth, said Mahavira, and India followed his path. His followers continued to thrive and practise his teachings. Over 2,500 years later, another Indian—Mahatma Gandhi—heeded Mahavira's advice and used ahimsa to overthrow the world's largest colonial power and lead India to freedom.

Mahavira's most important teachings were ahimsa or non-violence, the foundation of Jain ethics, and anekaantavada or many-sidedness, which creates an

atmosphere of harmony and removal of conflicts. He
is an icon for the numerous animal welfare movements
in India and elsewhere in the world, for he was the
first person to speak out against animal sacrifice and
cruelty towards animals and insist on vegetarianism.
He made the well-being of all life forms his primary
goal and philosophy and kindness to all living beings
essential for the liberation of the soul. Even today, it
is these principles that can ensure peace and harmony
in our conflict-ridden world.

LIVE AND LET OTHERS LIVE

Non-violence or ahimsa is the most important principle of Jainism. Mahavira taught that a good person should not cause any harm to another creature by thought, word or action.

Do not kill, do not cause pain.

Do not injure, abuse, oppress, enslave, insult, torment, torture or kill any living being.

Live and let others live.
Don't hurt anyone.
Life is precious to all living beings.

Non-violence means respect for all living beings.

If you cannot tolerate pain
from the words and deeds of others,
do you have the right to cause pain
to others through your words and deeds?

Non-violence and kindness towards living beings is
kindness to yourself.
For you are saved from sinning and
the consequent suffering.
Thus you can ensure your happiness.

Do unto others as you would like
to be done unto you.

Injury or violence caused to any life
in any form—animal or human—
is as harmful as it would be
if caused to you.

In happiness or sorrow, treat all creatures equally.
No living, sentient creature should be killed,
treated violently, abused, tormented or chased away.

Have compassion towards all living beings.
Hatred leads to destruction.

We cannot liberate our souls if
we put another life in danger.
Every living being has a soul—
it feels happiness and pain as we do.
Every living being wants to live peacefully—
it loves life as we do.
We have no right to destroy another life
or to cause its death.

We cannot achieve happiness if
we make another life unhappy, directly or indirectly,
intentionally or unintentionally.
That is the truth and we can experience this truth.

Sometimes people kill animals for excitement
or pleasure although
they know it is wrong.
Guilt and sorrow will overtake their joy.

Do not hurt another life, directly or indirectly.
You will only hurt yourself.

Violence cannot make anyone happy.

Violence is not a source of happiness.
When violence is stopped,
one moves to a higher plane.
This is the ultimate goal.

That sacrifice is the greatest
in which austerity is the fire, the self the fireplace,
exertion the ladle, karma the fuel, and
self-restraint and tranquillity
the oblations.

LIBERATE THE SOUL

Mahavira taught that the soul can be purified by destroying hatred and attachment. We are in control of our own destiny and can attain liberation. While he believed that there is no superior being or god who controls our fate, the soul follows the cycle of birth, death and rebirth until it reaches liberation.

What is the purpose of this universe?
Why is it here?
Why am I here?
Is it possible to liberate the soul?
There is no enemy outside your soul.
The real enemies live
inside you—anger, pride, greed,
attachment and hatred.

Every soul is omniscient
and blissful from within.
The bliss does not come from outside.
There is no separate existence of God.
Everybody can attain Godhood by
making an effort to liberate the soul.

The soul comes alone and
goes alone.
Nobody accompanies it and
nobody becomes its mate.

Every soul is independent.
No soul depends on another.

The soul must recognize its true self.

We shape our future
by our own deeds.
Good acts lift the soul to great heights, while
.bad deeds cause it to slide into despair.

Your destiny is in your hands.
No imaginary or external power
can help you.
Every living being wants to live and be happy.
Do not hurt or kill other living beings.
Rather, liberate your trapped soul.

One who is free of deceit is pure.
Only the pure attain liberation,
like a fire sprinkled with ghee.

Religion is the pond;
celibacy is its sacred shrine.
It is tranquil, with the serenity of the soul.
Having purified myself there,
I become pure, clean, cool and
devoid of impurity.

Once we know that 'I' am not my physical body
but a soul trapped within this body, we truly begin
the path to freedom.
Such freedom is bliss!

Misguided by the idea that
the physical body is 'Me', we carry
the burden of the body and
everything we possess.
We cannot experience freedom
as long as we carry this burden.
True freedom is freedom from this burden.

We believe wrongly that
someone else controls our destiny and
makes us happy or unhappy.
We alone, not some imaginary supreme power,
are responsible for our destinies.
We create our own misfortune
and become entangled in it;
we remain trapped within the painful cycle of
birth, death and rebirth.

Only we have the power to release ourselves
from sorrow through
our own efforts.
Awareness of this power

is self-realization.
When we realize this freedom, we understand
the difference between
the soul and its bondages.

Requesting favours from a supreme power
through sacrificial offerings or chanting mantras
is useless.
The power to liberate your soul
rests within you.

The differences in their karmic bondages cause souls
to take different births.
They are all capable of
attaining liberation, and must therefore
be equally respected and revered.

The soul is eternal. Neither was it created
nor can it be destroyed.
Every soul is independent and
creates its own destiny.

Our soul is imprisoned in our bodies
because of our karmas.
It is struggling to be free.

A living body is not merely flesh and bone,
it is also the abode of the soul.
The soul has the potential for perfect perception,
perfect knowledge, perfect power and
perfect bliss.

The soul brings both happiness and sorrow.
It is its own friend when it
treads the path of righteousness, and is its own enemy
when it treads the forbidden path.

There is no difference between the soul of an
elephant and that of an ant.

Through knowledge, the soul comprehends itself
as well as the external world.
This attribute of knowledge
is exclusive to the soul.

The soul is the abode
of all virtues, best among the substances
and supreme among all realities.

Souls are of three kinds—
external, internal and supreme.
The external soul is that which
is led by the senses.
The internal soul is that which
knows itself to be different from the body.
The supreme soul is that which has annihilated the
karmas and attained liberation.

The pure soul is
formless and free from
the activities of mind, body and speech.
It is free from conflict, detached, dispassionate,
unblemished, and free from
delusion and fear.

The jiva or soul is conscious, eternal, immortal,

formless and separate from the body.
It is the doer and the enjoyer of its actions.

The ajiva or non-soul does not know
either pleasure or pain,
cannot identify good and bad.

The soul is formless and invisible to the senses,
but it is eternal.
Attachment causes bondage, which is
the cause of worldly existence.

Karmas bind the soul.
A liberated soul is free from attachments.

By conquering all attachments,
one crosses the ocean of worldly existence.

CONQUER THE SELF

Mahavira believed that a person can be happy by controlling the passions of the self by practising meditation and penance.

Start practising control of the self with penance.
Begin with fasting.

Human beings are unhappy due to
their own faults.
They can be happy only by
correcting their faults themselves.

Silence and control of the self
constitute non-violence.

Just as a tortoise withdraws into its own shell,
a wise man should withdraw himself from evil
by spiritual exertion.

Just as a horse can be controlled by a bridle,
sensual pleasures and passions
can be overcome by
knowledge, meditation and penance.

As a manic elephant is controlled
and held captive by chains,
the unstable mind
is controlled and held captive
by the chains of knowledge.
Fight with yourself,
why fight with external foes?
He who conquers himself
will obtain happiness.

By being honest, a man achieves sincerity of
the mind, body and speech.
The five senses, the four passions—

anger, pride, deceit and greed—
and the unconquered self
are the ten mighty enemies.
When the self is conquered,
everything is conquered.

Harmony of speech and action
are achieved by sincerity.

If you want to cultivate a habit,
do so without any reservation until
it is firmly established.
Until it becomes a part of your character, let there be
no relaxation in your effort.

At the end of the day,
an awakened person contemplates thus—
what noble deeds have I done and
what have I not done? What good deeds remain
which I could have done
but have not accomplished?

Just as a person burdened by a load
experiences relief when he unburdens the load,
a seeker, by reviewing his wrong deeds
and confessing them
before his spiritual guide,
experiences lightness.

Retrospect on the day's events
regularly, at the same time
every day.
Irregular practices are not conducive to
the practice of retrospection.

Talk positive, behave positive,
act positive all the time.
Our actions are in our own hands.
Instead of trying to control others,
control yourself.
Instead of trying to win worlds,
win your inner self.

It is better to win over one's self than
to win over a million enemies.

We can be free only through
discipline of the self.
Self-discipline enables us to control and
eliminate ugly passions such as
anger, ego, deceit, lust and greed.

By controlling and conquering the self,
you will be liberated
from all miseries and sorrows.

Only one who conquers his own self
will experience supreme bliss.

One must conquer one's own self,
for it is difficult to do so.
One who does so is fortunate in this world and
will be in the next.

When the inflow of karmas through
the mind, speech and body is completely stopped,
the soul realizes itself to be
distinct from the body.

The dreadful tree of desires
brings forth dreadful fruits;
if this tree is permanently uprooted,
you can live peacefully.

The soul is different from the perishable body.
Steadily engage yourself
in destroying the karmic influence.

When a wrong deed is committed—
consciously or otherwise—
one must immediately desist and never repeat it.

How can one discipline others
when one is unable to discipline
one's own self?

The unprotected and unrestrained soul wanders
aimlessly in the world.
The careful and restrained soul
is liberated from all miseries.
Protect your self by
controlling the senses.

Whenever a wise man notices that
he is deviating from the path of righteousness
in thought, word or deed,
he should immediately
withdraw himself from that misdeed.

Destroy passion by observing austerity.
Relinquish the tendency of
enjoying the sensual pleasures.
It is better to control yourself through
self-restraint and austerity than
to be enslaved and subjugated by others.

An ascetic is one
who has total mastery over his mind.

The person who
eats food in excessive quantities
can never shine.

Those who take healthy food in small quantities
never fall sick and
do not need the services of a physician.
Do not consume food for taste or pleasure.
Regulate your diet for
religious pursuits.

ANNIHILATE YOUR KARMA

Mahavira taught his followers ways to annihilate one's karmas—by practising self-control and avoiding sinful activities. Only by doing this can one get rid of the karmas that have accumulated and attain liberation from the cycle of rebirth.

Nobody can escape the effect of their past karmas.

Attachment and aversion are
the root cause of karma.
Karma originates from obsession.

Karma originates from delusion and is
the root cause of birth and death,
which are the source of
all misery.

Attachment and aversion are two evils
that lead the soul
to commit sinful actions.
Ascetics who resist them
do not suffer during their lives on earth.

The soul wanders
through the cycle of birth and death
and is bound by eight karmas.
These eight karmas are
obstruction of knowledge, vision, feelings,
delusions, longevity, form, status
and power.

All beings wander and suffer
according to their previously acquired karmas.
Without experiencing the fruit of their karmas,
they will never be liberated.

One should give up sinful activities and
practise self-control.

He who is careless about
his physical activities and speech
and covets wealth and women
accumulates karmas of attachment and aversion
like an earthworm
collects mud in its body and mouth.

A self-restrained monk
annihilates his karmas accumulated
over several births if there is
no fresh influx of karmas.

Karma is the root cause of rebirth
and passions are the cause of karma.

All living beings owe their present existence
to their own karmas.
They are afraid of birth, old age and death.

Living beings are controlled by karmas.
But by taking action,
karmas are controlled by living beings.

Neither one's friends nor relatives
can share the burden of one's sorrow.
One has to bear one's sufferings
alone because karmas pursue only the doer.

Attachment binds the soul;
detachment frees the soul.

Past karmas will certainly
catch up with you in the future.

The ascetic cannot attain purification of mind if
there is no renunciation.

Right conduct quickly destroys accumulated karmas.

Once karmas are destroyed, the cycle of birth and
death will end.

Good thoughts which purify the mind
result in the annihilation of karmas.

The degree of attachment defines the
karmic bondage of a person.

Any spiritual practice by which
attachment is reduced and
karmas are annihilated
is the path of liberation.

CONQUER YOUR SENSES

Anger, pride, attachment, greed and such other longings of the senses keep the soul attached to the physical world. Only by being honest, humble and destroying desire can one overcome the senses and work towards peace and contentment.

One must destroy
the longings of sensual pleasures,
passions and the ego.

Anger, prejudice, thanklessness and wrong faith
destroy all the virtues
in a person.

One who is short-tempered,
ignorant, proud, harsh,
hypocritical and deceitful
drifts in the worldly current
as logs drift in a stream.

Conquer anger by forgiveness,
pride by humility,
deceit by honesty and
greed by peace.

He who is rid of delusion
destroys his sorrow;
he who is rid of desire
destroys his delusion;
he who is rid of greed
destroys his desire;
he who owns nothing
destroys his greed.

The mind of man is fickle.
He wants to fulfil all his desires,

which is as likely as
filling a sieve with water.

Banish all inauspicious thoughts
from the mind;
let auspicious thoughts flow
in from all directions.

ANGER

Anger destroys the self;
it destroys wealth, pleasure
and righteousness; it arouses acute hatred and
enmity and drags the soul
to lower existences.
Intense anger that lasts forever
drags the soul to hell.

When anger and other passions
get more inflamed,
character begins to decline.

One who is blinded by anger
does not hesitate to kill even his mother,
sister or children.

Anger is favourable to the enemy.
It brings grief to the person (who gets angry)
and to his relatives.
It defeats the person (who is angry) and
ultimately destroys him.

Just as a spark of fire destroys the stock of grains,
so also the fire of anger
destroys all the
divine qualities of a monk.

Anger spoils good relationships.

A person blinded by anger
loses good conduct and humility.

By conquering anger,
the soul attains forgiveness.

PRIDE

A person of humility is beloved by all.
Such a person acquires knowledge,
fame and fortune and meets with
success at every step.

Pride destroys humility.

Pride, which is like a pillar of stone,
prevents a person from being humble
and drags the soul to hell.
One who humiliates others out of pride
is ignorant.

DELUSION AND DETACHMENT

The most offensive enemy
does not cause as much harm
as do attachment and aversion.

If you desire to cross the terrible ocean
of worldly existence,

quickly board the boat
of austerity and self-restraint.

To attain liberation, one must
block the entry of karmas
through mind, speech and body.
One should neither commit sin,
nor cause it to be done,
nor approve of
the sinful activities of others.

Just as a little sourness
curdles milk,
attachment and aversion destroy an ascetic.
The tree whose roots are arid
will never flower,
no matter how much it is watered.

If delusion is conquered, the karmas
will never bear fruit.

A little water can extinguish fire.
But the waters of all the oceans
will not be enough to
extinguish the fires of
desire and delusion.

A person under delusion
suffers from
the cycle of birth and death.

Everyone knows of the acute suffering
of birth, old age and death;
but nobody develops detachment
from sensual pleasures.
How severe is the knot of illusion?

Shed all attachments
as a snake sheds its skin.

He who walks about unclad
and grows thin,
he who eats only once after

months of rigorous fasting,
if he is filled with deceit,
he will be reborn several times.

Illusion is enough to exterminate all truths.

Detachment controls the senses
as the mahout's hook
controls the elephant and
the moat protects the town.
To conquer the senses,
freedom from all possessions
is a must.

GREED

The more you get,
the more you want.
Desire increases with every acquisition.

Greed increases when
there is deceit and falsehood.

Just as a crane is produced from an egg
and an egg from a crane,
delusion springs from desire and
desire from delusion.

If there were numerous mountains of gold and silver
as large as Mount Kailash,
they would not satisfy a greedy man—
avarice is as boundless
as the sky.
This entire earth
with its crops of rice and barley,
gold and cattle will not satisfy
a greedy man.
Knowing this, one should
practise austerity.

Influenced by greed, a person resorts
to telling lies.

When greed is not controlled,
it sticks to the soul

like a permanent stain on cloth,
and drags the soul to hell.

By conquering desire,
you achieve peace.

Can one who is always greedy,
discontented and mentally unhappy
obtain happiness?

In adverse situations, others
take away the accumulated wealth.
The evildoer must suffer the consequences
of his evil deeds.

A person commits violence,
tells lies, commits theft and develops a yearning
for unlimited acquisitions
on account of greed.

Those greedy to amass wealth
cause more and more enmity.

External renunciation by a person is
of no use if his inner self
is bound with greed.

COMPASSION IS DHARMA

In conjunction with Mahavira's lesson on ahimsa or
non-violence is his wisdom about compassion. He
believed that every creature deserves to be treated
with compassion and love.

One day, as Mahavira sat in meditation
under a mango tree, two children
began throwing stones at it.
A stone hit the tree and a mango fell down.
When another stone hit Mahavira,
tears appeared in his eyes
The contrite children apologized,
'Sorry, it was a mistake.
We didn't want to hurt you.'
Mahavira replied, 'I am not hurt.

But when you hit the mango tree with a stone,
it gave you a mango; when you hit me
I have nothing to give you.
The thought brought tears to my eyes.'

Anger begets more anger.
Forgiveness and love lead to
more forgiveness and love.

Knowledge precedes compassion.

Noble conduct includes compassion.

A person who is compassionate to
all living beings and whose love
embraces the whole universe
gets auspicious karmas.

Purity in compassion is dharma.

A monk should be compassionate towards all.

Knowledge of the difference
between living and non-living beings alone
will enable one to be compassionate
towards all living creatures.

One who has a violent attitude
cannot be compassionate.

Simplicity, humility, compassion
and serenity are the four virtues
that enable the soul
to acquire a human birth.

HUMILITY IS THE ROOT OF DHARMA

Mahavira taught that having humility is essential to gaining knowledge and the route to dharma.

Humility is the root of dharma and
liberation the final goal.

From the roots of a tree develop shoots,
From shoots develop branches
and twigs.
Thereafter leaves, flowers and fruits
full of rich taste spring forth.

Restraint and austerity should
make a person humble and modest.
Righteousness and austerity are of no use
to a person who is not humble.

He who is modest
gains knowledge.
He who is arrogant,
fails to gain it.
Only he who knows this
can be educated and enlightened.

Learning with humility
is useful in this world and the next.
Just as a plant cannot grow without water,
learning will not be fruitful
without humility.

One who is obedient to his teacher
and is humble
crosses the ocean of birth and death
and attains liberation.

Humility is austerity and austerity is dharma.

THE FIRE OF MEDITATION

Mahavira taught that meditation was the way to calm
the mind's passions that lead to misery.

A steady state of mind constitutes meditation
while an active mind might be engaged
in either contemplation or
deep reflection.

A person who has no attachment,
aversion and delusion and
whose mind, speech and body are steadfast,
burns all auspicious and inauspicious karmas
in the fire of meditation.

The fire of meditation
destroys many karmas
in a moment.

Meditation is perfect when
the thought process is pure
and sublime.

A person whose mind is absorbed
in meditation is not perturbed by
miseries born of passions.

The fleeting mind, which is difficult
to control and conquer,
becomes still and peaceful by meditation.

To concentrate one's mind
upon one subject is meditation.
For monks who have concentrated
their mind on meditation,
it does not matter whether they stay in a densely
populated habitation
or in a secluded forest.

RENOUNCE SIN

Anger, pride, deceit and greed are at the root of all sins. Mahavira taught that one should give up these passions to live a life free of sin.

> At the root of all sinful acts
> is our passion for possessions.
> Cultivate forgiveness
> to eliminate anger,
> humility to control ego,
> honesty to avoid deceit and
> satisfaction to be free of greed.

> A life without passion
> is a life free of
> sin and bondage.

Sin sinks our soul in more bondage.
Violence is a sin.
Theft is a sin.
Lying is a sin.
Destroying another life
is a sin.
Even encouraging another
to hurt others is a sin.

Avoiding sinful actions makes
one absolutely happy.

When a sin is committed—
deliberately or otherwise—
one must immediately detach oneself
from the act, do penance and
resolve not to repeat it.

Anger, pride, deceit and greed
stimulate sinful actions.
One who desires the welfare of his soul
should renounce these four flaws.

THE LAST SERMON

The Uttaradhyayana Sutra contains the final sermon of Mahavira, who delivered 1,700 insightful sutras in seventy-two hours. A huge construction known as the samavasarana is believed to have been built by the celestial beings for this purpose.

> Just as the dry leaves of a tree
> wither away,
> so, too, does human life
> come to an end.
> Therefore, do not be careless
> even for a short while.

> As dewdrops last but for a while
> on the tips of kusa grass,

so, too, the life of man.
Therefore, do not be careless
even for a little while.

It is indeed very difficult
to acquire birth as a human.
One acquires it
after a very long time,
for the karmas that bind the soul
are very powerful.
Therefore, do not be careless
even for a moment.

Just as the lotus remains unaffected
by autumn water,
so, too, should you give up all attachments.
Therefore, do not be careless
even for a breath.

When you have crossed the mighty ocean,
why linger near the shore?

Hurry across, do not be careless
even for a moment.

Your body has become feeble,
your hair has become grey and
all your strength is depleted.
Therefore, do not be careless
even for a short while.

Whether in a village or
in a city, steadily proceed on the path
of peace with restraint and enlightenment.
Do not be careless
even for a second.

TO BE BORN HUMAN

There are four things of great value that are difficult
to obtain, said Mahavira: human birth, access to the
holy scriptures, faith in the holy scriptures and self-
restraint.

Not every human being has the opportunity
to listen to the holy scriptures and,
thereafter, to practise austerity,
forgiveness and non-violence.

Even after listening to
the scriptures, it is very difficult
to have faith in them, because people
often go astray, despite knowing
the right path.

Even after listening to
the scriptures and believing them, many people
who have faith in religion
do not practise it, making it difficult
to tread the path of righteousness.

Thus being born as a human being,
one must believe in religion and
follow it meticulously.
An ascetic should practise self-restraint and
annihilate his karmas totally.

Knowing all this, he who does not
walk the path of righteousness in this birth
as a human repents
at the time of death.

A person who wastes human life,
which is so difficult to attain and which is
as transient as a flash of lightning,
is not a noble person.

Ascetics who are always absorbed in
the contemplation of the self and
who pursue right knowledge, faith, conduct
and humility are
far superior to all others.

DETACHMENT AND AUSTERITY

Mahavira repeatedly said that material possessions should not be accumulated beyond immediate need. Attachment to material possessions and greed for wealth cause a soul to accumulate sin.

> Do not accumulate what
> you do not need.
> The excess of wealth in your hands
> is for society and you are its trustee.

> Even if this whole world
> full of wealth is given to a person,
> he will not be happy, for it is difficult
> to satisfy the greed
> of a rapacious person.

Wealth, possessions and grain
cannot relieve a person
from the bondage
caused by his karmas.

One should reflect that
one day, we have to abandon
all fortune, possessions, relatives
and friends and even this body and
depart from this world.

A person who knows that
wealth and relatives are incapable
of protecting him is
liberated from the bonds of karma.

Wealth cannot protect an imprudent person
in this birth or the next, just as
an extinguished lamp cannot
light the road.
Similarly, a deluded person cannot
walk the right path.

Ignorant people who earn money
through evil actions
earn the resentment of others.
They leave all their wealth behind
and go to hell.
A violent person does not understand
that life is perishable.
Being attached to worldly objects,
he dares to commit sin.
He toils day and night, assuming his body
to be imperishable.
He tries to earn more and more wealth.

Knowing that wealth is
the cause of misery and egotism,
root yourself in dharma,
which is unequalled and which
takes you to liberation.

He who controls the senses
and passions and concentrates on the self

through meditation and study,
he observes austerity definitely.

Fasting is good when
the person fasting does not have evil thoughts,
his senses do not become weak and
his mind, speech and body
are not damaged.

People who walk the path of knowledge,
faith, conduct and austerity
have a higher existence.

By observing austerity, one acquires
the ability to destroy karmas
and purify the soul.

Do not practise austerities
for this life or another.
Do not practise austerities for praise,
status, fame or name.
Practise austerities only to destroy karmas.

Living through an ordeal without protest
or self-pity and accepting life
as it comes is impossible
without equanimity.

GENDER AND CASTE

Mahavira saw no difference between people because of their gender or caste. He believed that a soul became great by its actions and that all souls were capable of great actions.

A person becomes great
by his own actions, not by his
gender or caste.

The real ornaments that enhance
the beauty of a woman are chastity and modesty.
All others are mere appendages.

A monk who does not flaunt
his family, lineage, caste, learning,

austerity, knowledge
and character practises humility.

Every person has been born
several times in high and low castes.
Nobody is either high or low.
Knowing this, who will experience
pride about taking birth
in a high caste?
And who will show attachment
to any particular caste?

YOU ARE NOT THE ONLY ELEMENT

According to Mahavira, all aspects of nature belong together and are bound together both physically and metaphysically. He emphasized the fundamental nature of symbiosis, or mutual interdependence between different life forms and the five elements—earth, air, fire, water and vegetation.

One who does not respect
the earth, air, fire, water and vegetation
disregards his own existence,
which is connected with them.

The most important principle of
the environment is that
you are not the only element.

The heart of a monk
is as pure as the autumnal waters,
as free as the birds
and as enduring as the earth.

A man seated on a treetop amidst a burning forest
sees all living beings perish.
But he doesn't realize that the same fate awaits him.
That man is a fool.

THE PATH TO LIBERATION

Mahavira preached that the true path to liberate the self is right faith (samyak darshana), right knowledge (samyak jnana) and right conduct (samyak charitra). An abhavya, who is unfit for liberation, may have faith and knowledge of the religion and even observe it, but this is done to attain worldly pleasures and not to annihilate karmas.

With knowledge one understands
the nature of substances;
with faith, one believes in them;
with conduct, one puts an end
to the inflow of karmas;
with austerity, one attains purity.

Without right faith, there is
no right knowledge;
without right knowledge, there is
no right conduct;
without virtues, there is
no destruction of one's karmas;
without destruction, there is
no liberation.

RIGHT FAITH

When one is totally absorbed
in contemplating the self,
he is said
to have right vision.

Right knowledge is of no use
in the absence of
right conduct.
Right conduct is of no use
in the absence of
right knowledge.

When a lame man and a blind man
are caught in a forest fire,
both get burnt
because the lame cannot walk
and the blind cannot see.
But when the blind and the lame help each other,
both manage to reach safety.

The desired result is attained when
there is harmony between right knowledge
and right conduct, for
a chariot cannot move with one wheel alone.

If a person has attachment, then
knowledge of all the scriptures cannot obtain for him
knowledge of the soul.
When he does not know the soul,
how can he know other substances?
When he knows neither the soul
nor other substances, how can he
be a person of right faith?

Defiled persons are those
who do not possess right faith.
They have no liberation.
Those who have given up right conduct
but have right faith may attain liberation by
practising right conduct again.
But there is no hope for those
who do not have right faith.

The value of right faith is much greater
than possessing all the treasures
of the three worlds.

The basis of all dharma
(righteousness) is faith.

A person without faith
is unfit for adoration and worship.
A person having right faith is one
who knows what is to be abandoned and
what is to be achieved.

If a person devoid of righteousness
undertakes severe austerities
for thousands of years, still he will be unable
to achieve self-realization.

RIGHT KNOWLEDGE

Knowledge is the most
important thing in life.
Knowledge precedes compassion.
How will an ignorant person distinguish
between good and bad deeds?

How can a person who
does not know the difference
between living and non-living substances
practise self-restraint?

It is the nature of the lotus leaf
to remain untouched by water.
Similarly, a righteous person
remains unaffected by passions
and sensual pleasures.

A person endowed with sacred knowledge
does not get lost in the world.

He who knows the self
to be wholly different from the body, and
knows it to be the knower
of all substances, is said to be
a master of all knowledge.

Knowledge of scriptures is
the supreme knowledge.

The mind is like
a furious elephant, but can be
controlled by the goad of
right knowledge.

Knowledge helps understand
the truth, controls the mind and
purifies the soul.
Perfect meditation destroys all karmas.
It is attained through knowledge.

By annihilating karmas, a person becomes liberated.
Hence, one should constantly acquire knowledge.

Knowledge is true and supreme,
for nothing can obstruct its path.
Its reach is far and wide.

After listening to the scriptures, a person
knows the difference between
good and bad deeds.
Knowing both, he should
practise that which will help him
reach the highest goal.

With knowledge,
one knows the truth;
with austerity,
one purifies the soul;
with self-restraint,
one gives up forbidden deeds.
The accomplishment of all three
leads to emancipation.

RIGHT CONDUCT

As the light from crores of
burning lamps is of no use
to a blind person, similarly the
study of numerous scriptures
is of no use to a person
who has no character.

Even limited knowledge of scriptures
is beneficial to a person
whose inner eye has opened,
just as the light of even one lamp
is enough to show the way
to a person whose eyes are open.

A person who is detached
does not enjoy sensual pleasures.
A person who may not be
sensuously experiencing them may suffer
due to attachment to them.
A person acting in a drama does not, in fact,
become transformed into that character.

A person who knows how to swim but
does not swim
when he falls into water will drown.
Similarly, a person who knows the path of liberation
but does not walk it
fails to cross his stay in this world.

Even a little knowledge will yield great fruit
if it is accompanied by right conduct.

Without good character,
a human birth is useless.

Right conduct includes compassion,
self-control, truth, non-stealing, celibacy,
contentment, right faith, knowledge
and austerity.

Renunciation of sensual pleasures
is right conduct.

Some householders are superior
to some monks in self-control,
but self-restrained monks
are superior to all householders.

The garb of an ascetic—lion-skin,
naked body, matted hair, tonsured head—
and other external manifestations
do not save a sinful ascetic.

He who has detached himself
from sensual pleasures
liberates himself in this life.

A person who renounces worldly pleasures
destroys his karmas,
and this leads to emancipation.

RIGHT WORLD VIEW

Do not believe that the universe
and non-universe do not exist.
They do.

Do not believe that souls
and non-souls do not exist.
They do.

Do not believe that dharma
and adharma do not exist.
They do.

Do not believe that bondage
and liberation do not coexist.
They do.

Do not believe that the effect of karmas
and their annihilation
do not exist.
They do.

Do not believe that there is
no attachment and aversion.
They do exist.

Do not believe that the four-fold existence
of births does not exist.
It does.

Do not believe that there is
neither liberation nor non-liberation.
They do exist.

Do not believe that there is
no abode of liberated souls.
It does exist.

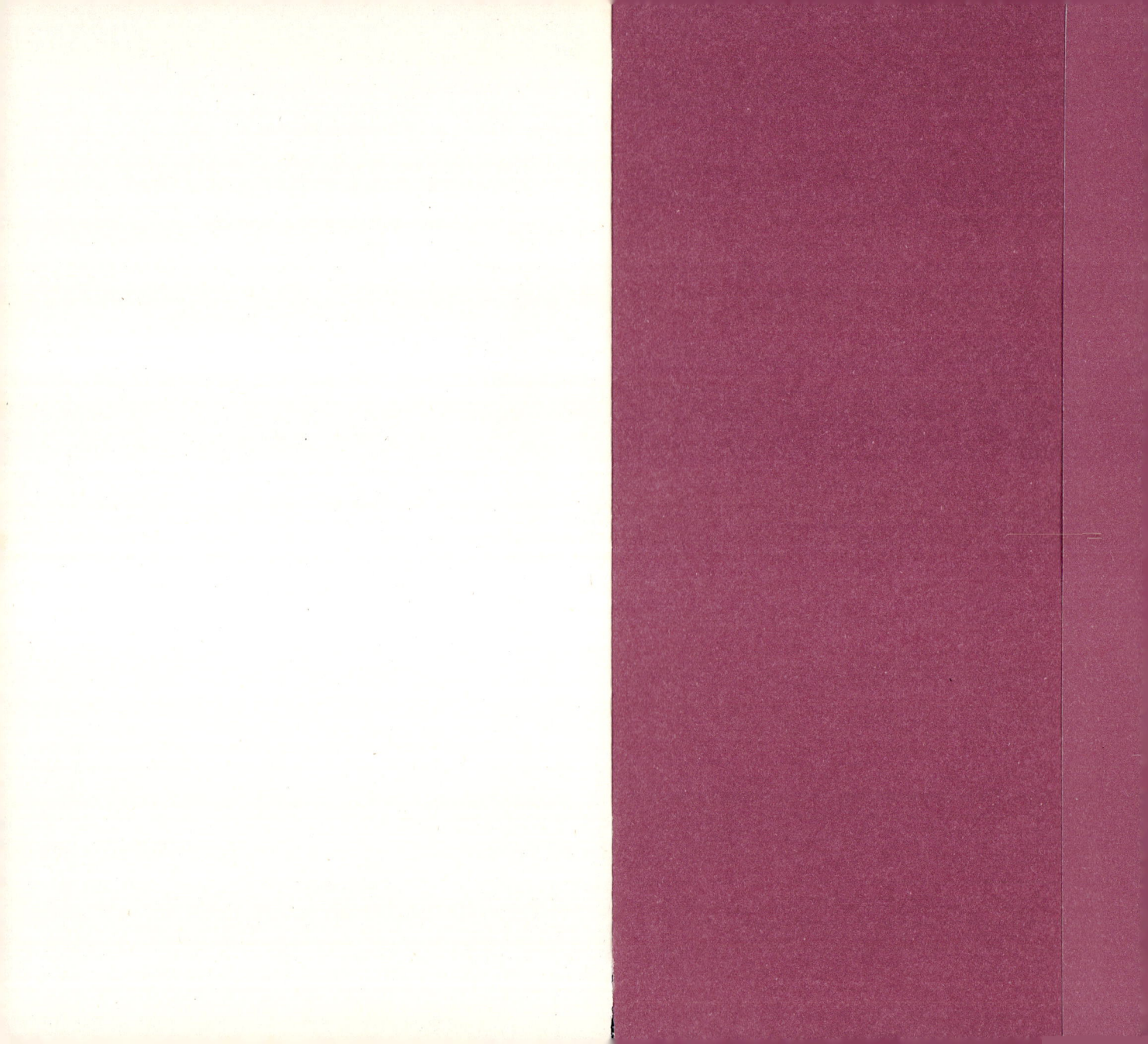